MW00873317

HAPPY Thanksgiving

This Book Belongs To:

_____

I Spy with my little eye
Something beginning with ...

Apple pie

I Spy with my little eye
Something beginning with ...

Basket

I Spy with my little eye
Something beginning with ...

Carrot

I Spy with my little eye
Something beginning with ...

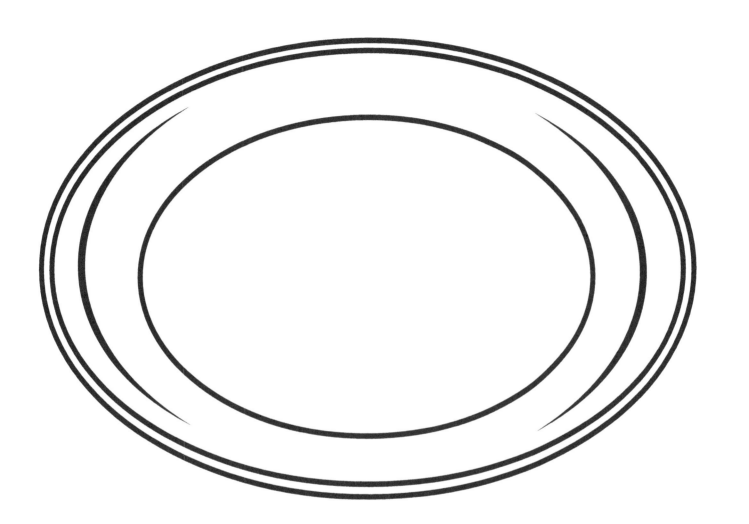

Dish

I Spy with my little eye
Something beginning with ...

Eggplant

I Spy with my little eye
Something beginning with ...

Fox

I Spy with my little eye
Something beginning with ...

Gravy

I Spy with my little eye
Something beginning with ...

Honey

I Spy with my little eye
Something beginning with ...

Ice cream

I Spy with my little eye
Something beginning with ...

Jug

I Spy with my little eye
Something beginning with ...

Kettle

I Spy with my little eye
Something beginning with ...

Lunch

I Spy with my little eye
Something beginning with ...

Meat

I Spy with my little eye
Something beginning with ...

Nuts

I Spy with my little eye
Something beginning with ...

Onion

I Spy with my little eye
Something beginning with ...

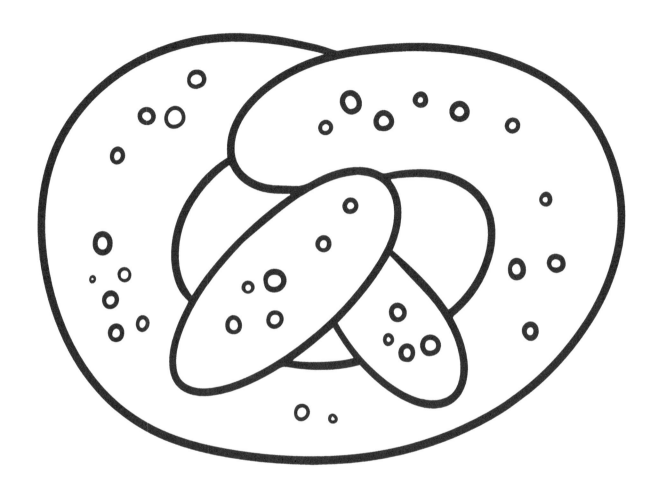

Pretzel

I Spy with my little eye
Something beginning with ...

Quill

I Spy with my little eye
Something beginning with ...

Roasted steak

I Spy with my little eye
Something beginning with ...

Sauce

I Spy with my little eye
Something beginning with ...

Turkey

I Spy with my little eye Something beginning with ...

Umbrella

I Spy with my little eye
Something beginning with ...

Vegetables

I Spy with my little eye Something beginning with ...

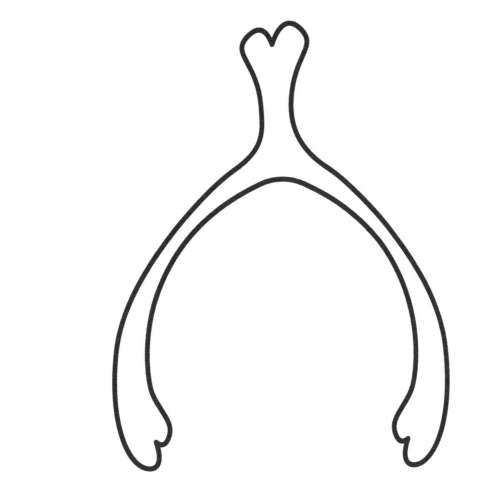

Wishbone

I Spy with my little eye
Something beginning with ...

Xerus

I Spy with my little eye
Something beginning with ...

Yarn

I Spy with my little eye Something beginning with ...

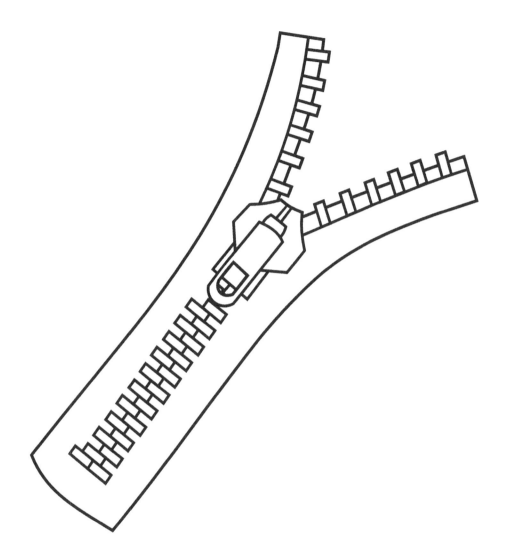

Zipper

I hope you enjoyed Leave us a feedback!

Click on our brand name and discover other children's books!

Made in the USA
Las Vegas, NV
02 November 2023

80078800R00059